14 STEPS

TO
LEGENDARY SUCCESS

AKHAND SWAROOP PANDIT

Published by :

Invincible Publication Pvt. Ltd.

Published by:
Invincible Publication Pvt.Ltd.
201A, SAS Tower, Sector 38, Gurugram, Haryana – 122003
Phone: +91-124-4034247, +91 9599066061
Website : www.invinciblepublishers.com

Sales Office : - 4760-61/23, Basement, Pratap Street, Ansari Road, Daryaganj, New Delhi - 110002
Phone: +91-11-40198405
Email: invinciblepublishers@gmail.com

This book is a work of fiction. Names, characters, places and incidents are either the product of the author's imagination or are used fictitiously.
Any resemblance to real persons, living or dead, or actual events or locations, is purely coincidental and the publisher does not hold responsibility for the same.

ISBN : 978-93-58865-74-5

Book Name : 14 Steps To Legendary Success

First Edition: October 2023

Contents

Dedication

To my dearest wife

You are the unwavering source of inspiration and support in my life. Your love and encouragement have been the guiding light that has fueled my passion for writing. This book is a tribute to your endless belief in my dreams and the boundless love that fills our every moment together. Thank you for being my rock, my muse, and my soul's truest companion.

STEP -1

Define success in your own terms?

> *"Define success on your own terms,achieve it by your own rules and build a Life you're proud to live."*
>
> ***- Anne Sweeny***

Success has so many meanings and for each person it means differently . For some, it is financial stability, while for others, it may mean getting that dream job. But the ultimate objective always remains the same: the desire to be successful. What takes to be successful? What takes to be happy about what you have achieved?

Let's find out in this chapter.

Once upon a time, two men, Aswant and Vineet, grew up together in a poor neighborhood. Their upbringing and their life had many similarities, however, one thing set them apart: it was the desire to become successful. Aswant was a talented young man and he was content with whatever he had. On the other hand, Vineet wasn't as bright as Aswant but had a strong drive to build a financially better life.

With time, both graduated from school and entered the real world. Aswant took over his father's mechanic shop and over the years grew it into a successful business. Though he wasn't a billionaire, he had a happy, loving family and was good at his job.

Vineet, on the other hand, pursued higher education. Eventually, he landed a well-paying job. He and his family leaped into a more comfortable lifestyle and Vineet finally achieved his dream of becoming financially independent. He was happy with his life.

Here comes the interesting part. When Aswant and Vineet were asked, "Do you think you are successful?" both had the same response.

"Yes, of course, I am."Their lives were very different and both Aswant and Vineet had contrasting ideas of what success meant to them. In their respective lives both believed that they had succeeded in achieving their goals and were successful.

So here comes the question folks - ***what is the definition of success?***

Almost every day, we hear success stories about all kinds of people. Mostly, these people tend to be CEOs, business owners, the chief managers of an organization, and others. We read about them in newspapers, follow them on social media, and wonder how they did it.

But take a step back and think: What does success even mean? Has anyone created a solid definition of success?

Does it mean money?

Does it mean fame?

Or does it mean absolutely nothing?

Let's simplify it. ***Being successful has a simple meaning, and that is achieving your goals***. These goals can be anything that you want - your desired financial numbers, a certain social status, power or even extended fame.

While the goals can be different, the process of setting them is pretty standard. And now comes the question:

How do I plan goals? Or, more precisely, which goals should I aim for in order to be considered successful?

Well, I cannot answer this question on your behalf. Why? Because only ***you can answer the question.*** Since every person thinks differently, they also aim for different goals in life. While some may define success with luxurious cars and houses, others may define it as happiness and joy. It may also mean being independent, paying your bills, and leading a simple and happy life.

While the notion of success may be popular, the meaning of success is personal. One needs to dig deep into their mind and soul to understand their needs. Take some time alone and think about it. Once you can define your goals and start working towards them, you will be able to find success eventually.

As I said earlier, everyone has different perspectives. So let me give you my perspective and tell you how I define success.

I come from a lower middle-class family. When I came to Delhi, I had just 1500 rupees in my pocket. My family never drove cars or bikes, I didn't even have a cycle of my own. When my cousins would get off of their cycle, only thenI would get a chance to ride a bicycle. Coming from a space like that, I associated success with my financial goals for a very long time.

For me, my aim was to make a lot of Money, buy a car, a house,and luxury commercial Properties for myself and my family. I felt a sense of pride when I paid for my younger sibling's college fees. As I started growing in my career, I succeeded in giving my family a sense of freedom from financial woes. Started making huge chunks of money through business,investments and real Estate properties.

I achieved the stage where my family could relax and enjoy their life because I was in a position to support them financially..

Now, there are two aspects to consider. First, with my success, I got to enjoy financial freedom and steadily achieve my goals. Second, my success extended to my family and enabled them to live a relatively carefree life. This aspect certainly made me happier and my success sweeter, giving me fulfillment as well.

Thus, in my words, the following is my definition of success:

Success means achieving desired personal goals, enabling your loved ones to lead a better life, and experiencing fulfillment along the way.

Now, it's perfectly okay if you have a different perspective. But, make sure that you are being true to yourself.

With my personal experience, I have come up with methods that will help you grow and eventually succeed:

1. Train yourself to have a growth mindset.

Renuka worked as an analyst in a multinational company. She was an intelligent woman and initially had no trouble getting promotions and pay raises. However, as time passed, she struggled to keep up with the industry and started falling behind. It took her a while, but she finally realized that intelligence wasn't enough; she had to keep an open mind and grow her knowledge constantly to stay at the top of her game.

While talent may help from time to time, during challenging times, your ability to improve yourself and grow will help you in achieving your goals. With hard work, focus, and dedication, nothing is impossible.

- Believe in your efforts and celebrate every step forward. If you've come this far in your journey, then there's no possible way anyone can stop you from moving forward.
- Keep an open mind for change to improve and prevent yourself from becoming stagnant and irrelevant.

- Learn new skills and be as agile and adaptable as possible. And even if you fail, learn from your experiences and move on. After all, failures are the stepping stones to success, aren't they?

2. Unleash your potential

When Nitin started working, he was overwhelmed by the competition and constant pressure of things. He shied away from challenges and only did what was required of him, nothing more. Soon, however, he realized people who started with him were climbing up the ladder, and he was still stuck at the bottom. So, he decided to stop holding himself back, and to his surprise, he got noticed and bagged a good raise.

Our brain is a source of unimaginable power and energy. While everyone has unique personality traits, leaders have a few specific ones that are common across individuals. Imbibe these traits and train yourself to follow them.

While it is natural for a human being to become comfortable in a particular set-up, it is necessary to take note of the changing world and be adaptive.

- Prepare yourself for the fierce competition you will face in the real world.
- Don't shy away from challenges and risks.
- Trust your gut, be positive, and make a priority chart to solve the problem.

- And most importantly, be ready to adjust. When situations become hard, step back, analyse, and train yourself to move forward, however slowly it might be.

3. Improve your willpower

Aman always dreamt of starting his own business. While he had everything planned out in his head, he procrastinated in real life and kept telling himself that he would do it someday, but over time, his dream started to fade. And one day, he realized that his dream had turned into just that, a fantasy built with clouds that vaporized before he could make them come true.

The most successful people in this world have one thing in common- they have a high level of perseverance and willpower. While some individuals naturally possess these qualities in their personalities, it's not impossible to cultivate and develop them by practice too.

To start, make small goals. Once you start achieving small goals by keeping at them, your confidence will grow. You can then set bigger goals and keep working to achieve them. Since you would have achieved smaller goals in the past, committing yourself to bigger goals becomes easier, even if they take more time. If you feel you're getting side-lined or find it challenging to resist temptations, then divert your attention and take a small break. After that, get back in, with guns blazing!

4. Strengthen your mental power

Anya barely passed her classes, and her teachers considered her a below-average student. Though Anya always wanted to be a pilot, her consistent low grades made her dismiss it as nothing more than a dream. One day, Anya failed a test. As she cried, her father consoled her and encouraged her to push her limits. And years later, when Anya sat in the cockpit, she smiled at the memory of her father's words and the day she realized the extent of her mental strength.

Our brain can cope with much more than we give it credit for. If you work on it and push the limits, you can manage much more than you think. While mental breakdowns are real and natural in high-pressure circumstances, it will be a great idea if you train and nurture your brain to manage and cope with your emotions.

- The first step would be to cut the negativity out of your life. Believe in yourself and encourage yourself to do better. Remember, you can rely only on yourself to do great things. And when you fail, because you will, keep pushing forward.
- Every failure is a lesson learned and wisdom gained.
- Most importantly, it is perfectly okay and normal to ask for help from time to time, no matter what society says.

- Say yes to therapy, psychological help, mentoring, and turn to friends if you wish to confide. A lot of mental pressure is released just by talking about it.

5. Be empathetic

Ishan was working for his dream job. He was well-paid, had an apartment in a fairly well-off neighbourhood, and even paid off his family's debts. Yet, he felt sad sometimes. When his job got overwhelming, or the stack of bills became more of a mountain, Ishan felt crushed but suppressing his feeling he forced himself to keep pushing forward. But one day, it became too much, and he broke down. After this incident, he started to acknowledge his feelings and make consistent time and efforts to decompress from the stress. Gradually to his amazement, his work and life improved drastically.

In this ever-changing world, we often find ourselves in tough circumstances. It is important to understand, analyze and reason with one's own emotions to keep a check on yourself and your emotional wellbeing.

- Always keep a check on your emotions and emotional well-being. It is okay to feel sad, depressed, or low, but it's not okay to dwell on them.
- Do not get comfortable in the darker end of the world. And when you feel frustrated or angry, release these feelings in the most appropriate and healthy ways instead of bottling them up. It is important to let off steam from time to time.

- Confide in friends, ask for help from mentors, and if necessary, seek professional help.

Success is simple. We complicate it unnecessarily with our own prejudice and by comparing ourselves with others. What I would suggest is that just keep two things in mind: One, your definition of success should be your own and two, it's only YOU who can make success happen for yourself.

Before you go to the next chapter, here is a small exercise for you. Write down any three things that you feel define success for you.

STEP -2

How do we measure success?

> *"You can't manage what you can't measure."*
>
> **- Peter Drucker**

People assume that the crossroads of life forks into two ways, left and right. However, in reality, you have the luxury of choosing from multiple intersections. Life gives us multiple options to choose from. Unfortunately, most people don't recognize those options and instead take the path that looks the safest- a path which many have already walked upon. ***But does this choice automatically lead to a successful and a happy life?***

Let's find out in this chapter.

To start with, let me share a small event of my life with you. As a motivational speaker and Founder of The Catalyst Group & Growfitz foods, I often get invited to colleges and other institutions to share my success story. It is always a pleasure to meet young and talented minds and talk to them about the nuances of my journey. Recently, I was invited to one such event and there I shared a small incident from my life. Here's an excerpt from the talk:

"As a teenager, I wanted to find an easy way out and

always wanted to have 'comfortable life'. I imagined a life wherein I wasn't struggling on a daily basis, and I wanted conveniences available at the instanceof a call. While these were reasonable demands that I had from my life, I wanted them right away. When the fulfillment of these desires delayed, it led to immense anger, frustration, and irritation. It is then that I started harbouring myself for my circumstances and my own self. As time passed by and one thing led to another, my hardworkfound a bit of peace for myself.

Even back then, when I used to think about my imaginary easy life, the figments were not my own. My parameter of a seemingly successful life was borrowed from the things and the people I saw around me. Seeing them live the 'ideal life' and having the ability to afford the latest gadgets and other fancy things. And all this made me want the same and more.

To achieve this, I took a path that was expected of me - I studied in a reputed engineering college, got a job during my course, slogged my days, and started working towards building the perfect life. This life looked perfect from the outside- a nice house, fancy gadgets,luxury cars, a happy family, and all that jazz. While all of this was great on the outside, I somehow became bored of the superficial and started looking for my true purpose . In the process I realized that material things give satisfaction for short term only and we as humans need something deeper to gain the contentment around success.

While wealth, possessions, and a fancy work title may look like measures of success to the society that you live in, they may not really make you Satisfied. Parental and societal pressure, coupled with bias, often work as impediments in realising what really makes us happy. Success is very personal- it ***must make you happy & content.*** If your measures of success don't make any sense to you, then it will make your journey of success very difficult, and unfulfilling.

Let's take the story of Raunak who visited his University as a successful alumni & speaker -

As Raunak faced the auditorium, his mind flashed back to his time in his college 20 years ago:bright-eyed and determined, Raunak worked hard to get placed on campus that would pay him a six-figure salary.

Shaking the memories back to the present, he turned to the students in front of him.

"Hello, students! It pleases me immensely to be back as an alma mater after all these years. Though back then, I was one of you, waiting impatiently for the guy on the stage to stop talking so that the actual event could start."

Laughter echoed through the hall.

"And since I'm still somewhat of an impatient fellow, I'll keep this short. When I joined this university, I didn't just do it because I was passionate; I did it because I thought it was the perfect path to success. And yes, I am successful. I got placed in a reputed company, paid off my student loans, and managed to settle my parents comfortably. But, never once did I feel content. No number of promotions or salary hikes made me happy. So, at the age of 25, I decided to quit my job and start my own business.

I faced a lot of criticism and backlash back then. To the outside world, I had the perfect life, on Earth would I give that up? But, choosing to quit that path gave me freedom. I no longer dreaded getting out of bed and was eager to face the day. Rejection didn't scare me; it pushed me to become better. And now, the same people who looked down on me admire me for following my heart.

So students, here is my advice: **There is no correct answer to success; it's different for everyone, and that's what makes it beautiful."**

As human beings, all of us have one ultimate goal which is to find happiness. But, that goal is often tempered with society's idea of success, and we end up thinking that the most used and common path would automatically make us happy. But is that really the case?

Over the years, I have realized that all of us are different and need our own measures of success. While the measures may vary, the way to find those measures remains the same. Here are different strategies that will help you find your way to build a successful life:

1. Find your life values

Before you start working towards success, you need to find things that are really important to you. It doesn't matter what social media trends say or what your friends feel is 'cool', The thing that matters is what makes you happy. Does a fancy work title make you happy Or does a 7-figure bank balance help you sleep peacefully at night?

- Find values that make you truly happy, and make sure you choose and fix your metrics.
- Once you find your metric, you should work towards it and sometimes you may even realize that you already have it.
- For example, a success metric could be to have a happy family and relationships that fill you with contentment. And sometimes one doesn't even realize that they already have it

Over time, you may also realize that what you have been working on does not fit with your metric of success. In that case, you can alter your course of action and lead a more fulfilling and peaceful life.

2. Stop Comparing

When I was young, my friends used to have huge bungalows and cars while I didn't have those luxuries. As a kid, I would often compare my situation with that of my friends. But, it was much later that I realised, they had other problems to be dealt with

As humans, we all tend to compare ourselves with those we know or sometimes even with others without knowing the other side of the story. We've all seen comparisons since childhood when we were compared to our friends, cousins or siblings. But does it make sense to compare? The answer is NO- in big blue neon light bulbs.

John Wooden, a successful basketball coach, said, ***"True success is attained only through the satisfaction of knowing you did everything within the limits of your ability to become the very best that you are capable of being."***

- Your only comparison should be with the person you were yesterday. But this also comes with caution- set realistic future goals for yourself.
- These goals may be tough but must be reasonably attainable.
- If you set impossible goals for yourself, you will end up disappointed, pushing you backward.

3. Your metrics must have a qualitative aspect

While setting tough goals and achieving them is wonderful, these goals should also be fulfilling and give you happiness. If these goals give you unwarranted stress, constant worry, and possible health scares, they are not worth it.

Life is to live, and the purpose of your goal is to enjoy the fruits of your achievement. If you remain unhappy even after achieving your goals, the whole purpose is defeated.

- Try putting your goals as a stick-on and follow it for the life you aim for rather than anything else.
- Try taking out some time for yourself.
- Be ambitious but Never to an extent that you compromise your mental health for your goals.

4. Be patient with success

The only thing you will get in today's world instantaneously is popcorn. If you wish to achieve your goals and the desired success associated with them, you will have to be patient.

- While success doesn't come to you overnight, it does come to you over time.
- It is easy to measure tangible results, but you must not ignore the intangible benefits you get throughout your journey.

5. Choose the kind of person you want to become

As time passes, our goals change and grow, and we too grow along with them. You must decide the kind of person you want to become. Which character traits do you want to imbibe in yourself? What kind of person do you see yourself becoming in the future?

Your actions today will make you the person you want

to be in the future. This will also help you make decisions when you are stuck in professional and moral dilemmas in your life.

Your pursuit of happiness will never truly end, but you must make sure you lead your life with confidence, passion, optimism, and commitment. Believe that your life matters in this unimaginably big universe. Remember, as long as your life's journey makes you happy, nothing else matters.

Before you go to the next chapter, here is a small exercise for you. Make a list of things that make you happy, and see if that matches with what you think will make you successful.

STEP -3

What does a success roadmap mean?

> *"A goal without a plan is just a wish."*
>
> **- Antoine de Saint-Exupéry**

Imagine you are running on a straight road without knowing where to go- what would happen? Either you'll get lost in the journey or you'll burn out without reaching anywhere.

Success - is a simple word that requires a lot of hard work and effort. However, mindlessly going down your chosen path will only cause frustration, irritation, and eventually failure. **Remember, hard work pays when done for the right aim**.

In this lesson, we will learn how to plan a roadmap to success.

Amaya was an ambitious young woman. When she was in second grade, she had her life planned out: get top grades, enter the best university, and get a high paying job. And for the most part, she was successful. She ranked number one in her district, and even got admission into the best university in her state.

But, things seemed to go downhill from there. She

found that her classes didn't interest her, and she often felt lost. As the feeling of drifting along increased, she took a step back and reevaluated her plan she had made for a successful life.

This time, she factored in her interests, circumstances, and short-term goals while mapping out her future goals. And when she put into action, she was able to get her life back on track.

When questioned later about the change, Amaya's response was short and to the point.

If your plans for success are stagnant, then your life will end up the same way.

Before defining a success roadmap, it is also essential to define what success means to you. Success is a relative term, and the definition can be personal to each individual. For some, it may be a powerful position, while for others, it could be a million dollars in the bank account, fast cars, or lavish homes. Or it could simply be the ability to choose and having enough time to do what they want.

So what is a success roadmap?

A success roadmap is the creation of your success journey with the destination visible to the eyes of our minds. Think about your childhood dream or vision and if it still holds true for you. Defining success in materialistic or monetary terms is often a mistake or a narrower view of the broad-based term like a success roadmap.

When we define our goal for success, we also want to think about the steps we take to achieve it. These steps can be defined as a success roadmap. We can also call defining our goal as a first step on this roadmap.

A success roadmap is like a life plan which can be achieved with definitive strategic planning. It is also a tool for communicating your life plan on the road to success. A roadmap is important for any aspect of your life, whether personal or professional, as it makes sure you are in the driver's seat of your life.

A good roadmap will entail a strategic plan along with a communication tool and a high-level document that helps you think, plan, strategize and execute a long-term plan to achieve the goals you have set for yourself.

You can create a written roadmap, visual roadmap or a combined roadmap so that you have something tangible to fall back on. A lot of times, overconfidence makes us think further than our actual capabilities and that becomes a roadblock. To overcome this, it is important to work in a framework or a quadrant format to know and understand your strengths and weaknesses. This exercise will help you plan better.

However, people often mistake it for a rigid roadmap and do not look beyond it. In reality, it is like an actual road map where we sometimes have more than one option to reach our set destination, and just like the application, it will show us multiple options along with the time it will take for us to arrive at the destination.

Similarly, we have to be flexible enough to think and create multiple ways of successfully reaching our destination of success.

So, how do we create a roadmap?

With proper research and insight, it's quite easy to create a success roadmap for yourself. The steps to be taken to create a successful roadmap that gives you your desired results are:

✧ Take stock of your life

It is important to analyze your life and take stock without any bias. Your loved ones may be able to help you, but only you would know yourself the best. You need to have an eagle's view, which will help you recognize the areas that need work and your areas of strength. Harsh criticism or too much leniency with yourself will not help as both could create a negative thought process in your mind.

✧ Brainstorm your possibilities

The next step is to brainstorm all the possibilities with minute details to create a blueprint for your roadmap to success. You need to be strict with yourself and have a very disciplined approach to set the tone right from the beginning. Writing and creating thought bubbles will help you. Taking your mentor's help at this stage can also help see possibilities you may have missed.

✧ Create a Plan

We don't want to create a ''back of the envelope'' kind of plan, that is vague or ambiguous. We need a full-fledged, detailed written plan fleshed out with every minute detail. Working with SMART is the best way to work out those details without getting lost in them.

» S – Specific

The goal should be specific, and you should be clear on why and how you will achieve it. Plan out the details and map out our goals thoroughly and precisely.

» M – Measurable

Your progress at each step should be measurable, including mini targets and goals to attain on your journey towards the main success roadmap. This milestone will indicate whether you are moving in the right direction or not.

» A - Attainable

We often set ourselves for unattainable goals that fall short. In both these situations, we are disconnected from reality, making our goals difficult to accomplish.

» R – Relevant

The roadmap and the final destination should be relevant so that success becomes more plausible. It should make sense when measured against the area you are working in.

» T – Time-Based

Like any journey, you cannot be out open-ended or meandering. In the same way, a success roadmap cannot be vague. It must have binding factors like time and effort so that you can measure your success and achievement. Also, monitor your growth keeping your ultimate goal in mind. Prioritize your life and set your goals.

✧ Check your mental and physical health

To achieve success in any field of life, you need to be healthy physically and mentally. Otherwise, you will never reach where you want to be. A healthy mind and body will propel you towards your goals and ensure you are always on track of your roadmap.

✧ Review your roadmap regularly and correct course when required

We often forget to review our growth or the path we are walking on because we have our eyes set on the goals. Regular reviews on set days are vital for you to correct the course. You can do so by rewarding yourself for every small milestone you achieve. This will also help you to check things that are not working out for you.

Making a roadmap and sticking to it should be a part of your habit, this will get you greater success in all aspects of your life.

Be flexible, adaptive and innovative to keep your path open and receptive to achieve higher and faster success..

Before you go to the next chapter, here is a small exercise for you. Make a list of your goals, and create a road map with every detail for the same.

STEP -4

How to develop smart hacks for yourself

> *"We all have two lives. The second one starts when we realize we only have one."*
>
> **— Confucius**

There are no shortcuts to success, but there are tricks and hacks you can use to manage your time essentially and effectively. While hard work is important to achieve your goals, it is equally important to work smart in order to develop and grow. Using them, we can make our lives easier and focus on our goals with a clearer head. ***As long as shortcuts help us work smarter, you can use them to march towards success.***

Let's find out more about the different types of hacks in this chapter.

Ritvik was a hard worker. He was the topper of his school and spent all his time studying to keep his marks high. He was working day in and day out but slowly he started to burn out. Constantly studying, memorizing, and taking tests were beginning to take a toll on him, and soon, his performance started going downhill. Frustrated by this, Ritvik was at his breaking point, this is when his dad gave him some advice. His father advised him to be smart about his work and use easy hacks to handle things better. Though initially skeptical about using 'hacks' and 'shortcuts', he soon found himself working more efficiently and without getting stressed .

While working hard is a no-brainer to achieve success, **using life hacks and shortcuts to work smartly is also necessary. THe combination of working hard and smart will help make your life easier without compromising on the quality of your success**.

Life hacks are little tricks, shortcuts, or novel methods to boost your productivity. These little tricks will help you increase your efficiency in all aspects of life. The smart hacks movement was started by computer experts, who were known to suffer from information overload or by people who would love to work smartly in order to finish the same task that might usually take hours.

Hack, conventionally, means to cut with a rough or heavy blow. Today, it describes an effective solution used in a not-so-nice manner to get your work done, especially in a computing problem or shell scripts or in the command lines. This term has extended its use in colloquial terms of a life hack to solve any problem an individual faces while doing their work. Life hacks also help change your habit or do something important that you are avoiding.

The term life hack was first used in the O'Reilly Emerging Technology Conference in San Diego, California, by journalist Danny O'Brien. Later, O'Brien and blogger Merlin Mann co-presented a session "Life Hack Live" at the same event. Consequently, they co-authored a column by the same name. By 2011, the word 'life hack' was added to the Oxford Dictionaries.

Why are life hacks important?

Life hacks are important for the simple reason that they make our lives easy. If a trick or a shortcut helps us make easy and smart decisions or makes it convenient for us to follow a good habit, then why not use it? You just need to know how to use the right hack at the right time.

At the same time, we should keep in mind that hacks won't work for everything in life. Not all solutions or tricks can be the same for all. Therefore, it is important to develop hacks that work for you exclusively. Life hacks are just a way to do something for a short period. We cannot keep using them as our needs, problems, and life will change constantly. Thus, we need to adapt to that change and keep innovating with the hacks.

Some people think that life is a set of complex problems and we need to find solutions for them at all times. However, this may quickly become an obsession concerning means rather than the end.

Life hacks are not for avoiding issues. Rather, they are to be used to find smart solutions to resolve them and get back to things that make us happy. Life hacks are good solutions to finish all the mundane tasks of life so that we have more time to pursue our creative endeavors and work on our goals. Sometimes people use these hacks the other way around and use them to reach their goals faster and suffer in the end. We cannot hack our lives, but we can create life hacks to help us solve our pestering life problems to get back on track.

What are some life hacks that I can use?

Life is a series of decisions that we take. No matter right or wrong, they will surely take us somewhere. We need to stop obsessing over making the right decisions at all times and enjoy the process of making a few wrong ones too. In fact, the latter are the ones that will take us back to our right path or maybe show us a shorter one. We do not create the life of our dreams by making the right decisions; a progression of smart decisions helps us create what we want. We can succeed by focusing on the things that matter and leaving the rest. Here are some life hacks that will help you make better and smarter decisions in life:

1. Stick to your mission

We live in a world with many distractions. We also go off track by micro-managing or spreading ourselves too thin in our work. If we wish to succeed, we must stick to our mission and let the rest be taken care of by those who know their work well.

2. Avoid decision exhaustion

We make hundreds of decisions in a day. Some are trivial, and some are big, but constantly being on that boat will harm your focus. Like the famous life hack of Steve Jobs and Mark Zuckerberg to wear only a particular type of clothing every day, we can also reduce our time spent on trivial matters by either clubbing them together or making a firm decision about it.

3. Work with deadlines

When you start a task, decide the time you want to spend on it and stick to it. Doing this will help you focus better on your current task, and you won't let your mind wander.

4. Learn to recognize patterns

There is a pattern to our lives each day; try and recognize it. After that, stick to what works for you and let there be a natural flow of said events. Doing so will help you be better prepared as you will know how much you have on your plate.

5. You cannot control everything

You can only work on the things that are under your control. Worrying or trying to control things out of your reach is a complete waste of time and energy. The more you focus on the task at hand, the better you are equipped to make faster decisions and keep the focus on your goals.

6. Make a predetermined number of decisions

Commit yourself to make only a set number of small and big decisions per day. If you are done for the day, keep the pending decisions for tomorrow.

7. Always think of an alternate or reversal of the decision

It is always better to make decisions that can be altered or reversed, though we know not all decisions can be reversed. It is essential to keep this in mind while making major life decisions. While making a business decision, make sure to evaluate them and have the ability to reiterate them.

8. Use common sense more often

Sometimes, we need that one push for ourselves to send us in the right direction. And that one push can be from anyone; for example, a friend who understands us.. It is important to decide once and not doubt your decision later.

9. Be ready for uncertainty

We are never 100% sure about anything even after the decision has been made, and we are awaiting its results. We have to be ready for the uncertainty of the situation and not fret over it. We may have to expect that we may be wrong, but that doesn't mean we can be indecisive at all times.

10. Do not give into self-doubt

A lot of the time, we let our self-doubt take control of our lives while making a decision or after it too. Never let yourself in a situation where your self-doubts paralyze you in any way.

11. Do not be a victim to analysis paralysis

We also analyze, collect and speak to so many people before making one life-changing decision that by the end of the multiple Google searches and pep talks with our loved ones, we still end up being unsure and undecided. Be clear about what your end result should be, and take inputs with them in mind.

12. Respect others opinions too

We all think, perceive and experience things differently. Therefore, do not blindly reject other people's opinions and At the same time, do not decide entirely on that basis. Consulting a friend before an important decision is okay, but complete dependency on their thoughts and opinions is dangerous.

Life hacks are about small things. It can be as simple as ''what clothes do I wear today'' or much more complex decisions. We have to decide which life hacks will help us make better decisions or set better goals for ourselves so that we do not lose track of the important things in life.

Before you go to the next chapter, here is a small exercise for you. Make a chart and divide them into big and small decisions. Once that's done, figure out which life hacks will work best for every decision.

STEP -5

How to move from failure to success?

> *"Only those who dare to fail greatly can ever achieve greatly."*
>
> **- Robert F. Kennedy**

No, this chapter is not about failure or handling failure. This chapter is about how to use failure as a stepping stone to success. Trust it or not, failure is a step towards success. Failure, in fact, is like that bitter medicine which tastes bad but helps you get better. Failure is bitter, painful, and has the power to make us give up everything we work for. But, without failure, we will never truly understand the sweet, wonderful feeling we get when we achieve success. Like yin and yang, without failure, you can never achieve success.

Let's learn the importance of failure in this chapter!

Naina felt frustrated. As she ran the code for the billionth time, she leaned back and rubbed her eyes. The program she was working on was her pet project, and for the past few months, she had put all her efforts into making it work. Only, she was stuck with a recurring error for the past two days, and she could feel her disappointment setting in. When the code failed again, she groaned and felt tempted to give up, tired of failing over and over. However, just as she was about to shut down her laptop, she heard her mother's voice in her head, reminding her good things would happen to those who never give up. Feeling a surge of determination, she rolled her sleeves and dove into the world of coding once again. And the next morning, surrounded by 10 cups of coffee, Naina whooped gleefully when her code ran successfully.

Most often than not, the path to success is always sketched out by the society- what is good, what is not productive, what will make us successful- everything is told to us. Right from the 1st standard, we know that getting 100% is successful and getting anything lesser than 40-50% is not successful. Right from childhood, we are taught to run behind success and failure is presented as such a monster that you learn to be scared of it but no one ever tells us the importance of failure.

Few years back, I met an entrepreneur while traveling. She was a topper since school, did extremely well at studies in college and was supported throughout with her family business funds. For the world, she was extremely successful. But when I spoke to her, she mentioned how not having exposure to failure in her early startup days made it tough for her.

I still remember what she said,

"You know, in the early startup days when there was any failure, I had the padding of my family's business.

But I feel I should have handled it independently, faced failure and then should have come out stronger."

"But, why do you say so?" I asked.

"Because today when there are bigger challenges, I feel stiff- as if I am unable to deal with it. People feel success is a great teacher. I don't agree. It's failure that teaches you the most." She responded.

Her perspective was interesting. Failure indeed is a great teacher.

Now, that doesn't mean you go and fail deliberately. But yes, when even after trying hard, you don't succeed, take that as an opportunity to learn.

For decades, the main ingredient missing in the recipe of success is the exact opposite of what we seek: failure. Often, as humans, we live through everyday problems and just focus on the positives, and society embraces success stories with open hands while its antonym is treated with disdain.

But the question here is, what are the prerogatives for positives?

Let me simplify this for you.

As the saying goes- "Life is what you make it" Fashioned by the high-achieving society we live in, failure is often perceived as the worst circumstance, and instead of embracing it, we make it our obstructive nemesis.

But then you might think, what good does come from failing? Why is it important?

While it is quite understandable that putting yourself out there while feeling stuck and getting bruised is no fun, it is also necessary to understand that tribulations in life can be agony or triumphs, depending on how we choose to deal with them.

"A smooth sea never made a skillful mariner".

This is, in fact, the truth of any success story. Just as hard work is the key to success, failure is the highway. In all honesty, failure is a disciplinarian whose lessons are no fun, and we heartily desire to overlook it. However, to achieve success, we need to embrace and learn from these lessons. In fact, we need failure as it is an important tool that aids in moving ahead. As Tom Watson rightly said,

"If we want to succeed, we need to double the lesson that failure teaches."

And indeed, failure has many lessons to knock with at our door. For it is when we fail we recognize where we need to put in more effort. Failure, with the razor-edged pain, agony, guilt, and regret, makes us stronger and helps us bounce back. It is again failure that makes us realize that to achieve greatness, to live in the competing world, we need to struggle and gain strength on our way. Failure is the leverage to the same.

Life Experiences to Learn from

Having said that, before I get into embracing this indispensable amenity for our voyage into success, here are some life experiences of people who embodied all the setbacks to come out with overwhelming triumphs. These aren't just stories of great failures; these are stories that helped me keep going when everything seemed bleak.

When an old man's journey inspired everyone: The first story about failure turning to success is the life history of a notable man. At the age of sixty-seven, the workshop of Thomas Alva Edison, established with hard work, was lost to fire. Standing at the point of old age with little insurance for his lifetime effort, this great American inventor turned a major obstacle into a life lesson for eternity. Watching his establishment burnt to smoke, he acknowledged the obstacle thrown his way as a new opportunity to start a new and correct old mistakes. Following this incident and turning the setback into a comeback, Thomas Alva Edison invented the phonograph.

When Obstacles became the staircase to success: Another historic piece of evidence is the story of Abraham Lincoln. It makes me realize that success is not a journey without failure. Rather, success is the journey of overcoming it with experience and strength to move ahead. Abraham Lincoln's life was full of obstacles. Starting from a young age when he lost his mother, his tribulations continued with failed businesses, defeat in a legislature race, and losing his beloved at the age of twenty-six. Followed by mental illness (nervous breakdown) and losing his senatorial race at forty-nine, he could have quit at any point. However, rather than quitting and giving up on the sourness in life, Lincoln embraced all his failures and proceeded to become the 16th President of The United States at the age of fifty-two.

The life history of these great men only confirms the message that failure is as important a foundation of success as hard work and persistence. In fact, success is more about embracing the obstacle and doing the small things with great effort.

So, to put it in a refined way, it is important to understand that failure is a detour and not a dead-end in our journey to success.

Transition From Failure to Success

While it's not easy, once you start embracing your failures instead of rejecting them, the path to success becomes easier to handle. Here are some techniques I used in my journey to beat the odds and move ahead from failure to success with strength. As Henry Ford said,

"If we think we can, we really can, and if we think we cannot, we cannot".

✧ Change the mental model

To begin with, the stepping stone in the long journey

of building our success story is to change your outlook. For years, failure has been belittled by the high-achieving fast phased society, and it only recently has taken on a counterintuitive luster.

- However, to make your journey from failure to success, the first thing you need to do is acknowledge the elephant in the room.
- Failure is inevitable. And to succeed and reach your best and come out more skilled, failure should be acknowledged. Change your outlook; failure is not between you and your dreams. Instead, it's with you and pushing you ahead to reach your goals.

2. Accept, then move on.

Once you accept failure as a part of your journey, the next step is not to dwell. Past needs release. Simply put, learn from your mistakes; they don't define you as a person. That will happen only when you live in that place and repeat the same catastrophic mistakes.

- So, sit back, reflect and understand the failed experience.
- Following this, brush yourself and move ahead. Dwelling creates a web of gloom. The more you dwell on your failures, the stronger the web will start shading your mindset. Remember, a positive mindset is not about overlooking or jumping from your mistakes. Rather, it is about being more solution-focused.

3. Learning from your mistakes

Problems and failures are part of our life; they are inescapable. That is, in simple words, nothing will ever come easy in life. Our goals will test our grit constantly, and it is on us to make the best of the given situation.

- Therefore, to move from failure to success, learn from your mistakes, and change your focus to understand that failure is the opportunity to grow.
- Failure is the best teacher; acknowledge it and turn yourself into a curious person. Use failure as your guide about where not to venture and buckle up to come out with a greater strength.

4. Don't hold back from starting anew.

Failure is not an obstacle. Rather, it is the stepping stone towards the journey ahead. Triumphs in life do not come without effort. However, time and again, you may stumble, and sometimes, your efforts may fall short. But this is where you need to understand and instill the secret of success.

- You need to realize that success is not really about how high we go; it is about our ability to bounce back every time we stumble. So, no matter how many times you fall, pick yourself up, take help, get yourself together and start anew.

In the end, it is important to understand that the more obstacles you face, the sharper you come out. People who have failed are more secure than those who have never faced a failure. All you need to do is upgrade your narrative towards these stumbles, for every success story is built on the foundation of mistakes. Embrace your failures, and turn a setback into a comeback, as success is not about doing great things; it is doing the small things in great ways.

Before hopping on to the next chapter, just do one thing, let go of your fear of failure. Go, achieve your dreams fearlessly!

STEP -6

How to Train Your Mind?

Developing inner values is much like physical exercise. The more we train our abilities, the stronger they become. The difference is that, unlike the body, when it comes to training the mind, there is no limit to how far we can go.

- Dalai Lama

It's easy to plan your goals and dream of achieving success and all the benefits that come along with it. However, unless you have a strong mindset to achieve your dreams, they will always be castles in the air. The most important step to achieving success is to train your mind for the same. Your mind is your biggest weapon, and like all other weapons, it must be sharp all the time.

Let us find out more about different ways to train your minds in this chapter.

Manu watched the sunset wistfully lost in thought. Leaning back in her chair, she looked back on her eighty years of existence and once again felt the familiar sense of disappointment. As a child, she had big dreams. She always used to say she would have a huge mansion and a great job. But they never came true. As she grew older, she continued to dream but never put her mind to working towards them. And one day, she realized that her dreams were nothing but clouds in the sky.

Though she wished she could go back and change her life, Manu knew she couldn't. Thus, she made sure her kids' mindset was trained to work towards their goals and make their dreams come to life.

Our mind is a powerful tool. No matter what your goals are, whether it is to chase happiness or whether it is to go after money, your mind is your best ally. However, it won't be your most faithful ally if you cannot train it to do your bidding. I'm sure everybody has heard the phrase, "an empty mind is a devil's workshop." There is, however, only a little truth to that saying. You see, even an empty mind, if trained well, will never wander away from your true being.

It was Frederick Lenz who said,

"By disciplining and training the mind to focus on one thing, we gain control of perception. We learn to grab it and put it somewhere we want it to be."

Ultimately, training the mind means commanding it to perceive a situation or a scenario the way you need it to be perceived and then taking action to follow through on that perception.

Before we get into actually training our mind, we need to truly understand what we want to train it for. There is really only one way we can know our ultimate goal for training our minds – deep introspection.

What is your goal? What is it that you're chasing?

The truth is, once you figure out the answer to that question, you have already completed 50% of your mental training. Most people get stuck at this point. Indecisiveness and a lack of faith in one's ability generally begin to do the Devil's bidding and prevent you from getting closer to your goal. So, the first action that you must take is to push through the inertia. A hack to do this is to simply note down your thoughts. Doing so realizes your desires and offers a reference point far more reliable than the untrained mind.

A simple question that has probably popped up in your thoughts is,

Why do I need to train my mind ?

You have come this far in life without any specific mental training. So why now? What does the effort of training my mind offer me now?

Simply put, in Robert Frost's words,

"You have a long way to go before you sleep." And that sleep must be a peaceful one.

Yes, you have come this far. But have you thought about how much further you want to go? Have you thought about your potential, which you can unleash if you push through that inertia and intractability of your mind to achieve things you never even dreamt of achieving? Please understand, at this point, that training your mind is not for the weak-hearted. Training your mind requires persistence. Training the mind is what allowed great people like Dr. A.P.J. Abdul Kalam and Stephen Hawking to be as great as they were. Otherwise, how could a poor child with a bleak future become one of the greatest men India ever saw? How would a 20-year-old, freshly diagnosed with Motor Neuron Disease, become one of the greatest scientific minds humanity ever had the privilege of knowing?

Having said that, there are some techniques I have found extremely helpful in my journey to beat the odds stacked against me. Of course, these are experiential learnings that are based on the teachings of great minds all over the globe. Technically, if you stay committed to the goal of having a fully trained mind, you will achieve it.

1. Meditate

Meditation is one of the most underestimated tools in a human's arsenal against mental issues. But what is meditation? Meditation is simply 'being.' It acts as a conduit for your mind to enter a safe space where your thoughts can flow like a river. Once they have flown, there is nothing but stillness and peace.

Meditation is not easy, but can be: Contrary to the intuition that meditation is easy, allowing yourself to simply be is an ordeal, especially for the untrained mind. In fact, when you're a beginner in this practice, you will want to avoid negative thoughts and merely focus on the positive. However, remember that meditation is a way for your body and mind to remove these unwanted information by allowing them to flow freely rather than avoiding them.

The five magical minutes: My suggestion is to take out at least 5 minutes from your day and relax. Allow your thoughts to flow. At the end of those 5 minutes, you will have the clarity you didn't realize was possible.

Now, the crucial thing to remember is that this clarity is short-lived when you're starting. It takes years for most people to achieve a stable mind capable of allowing that clarity to persist. But practice makes it perfect, and as long as you stay persistent with this practice, you will be able to sustain that clarity.

2. Know the difference between thought and action.

The clarity that meditation offers serves a larger purpose. It allows you to introspect or think with a fresh, and a better perspective.

- **Thinking is not enough:** Simply thinking about your plan of action or the situation does not guarantee any results; you must take action using this fresh perspective.

- **Do it:** Take an example, you are unhappy with your fitness level and want to improve it. Thinking about this does help you find the motivation. However, if you push past the inertia of your untrained mind and pen down a plan to improve, your motivation will bear results.

- **Force your mind to act:** Force your body to act. Your acts will ultimately give you the result that you want. If your body cannot respond to your mind, your mind simply isn't strong enough to make your body respond to its commands. Therefore, it is crucial to strengthen that resolve over time.

3. Take a breather

Last but not least, the journey to a fully trained mind is a long and arduous one. And along the way, there will be opportunities to defect or, at the very least, digress from your goal. It is at times like these that your mind should reset.

- Take a breath. Look at your scenario from a neutral perspective. Allow your mind to venture just far enough with your thoughts for you to be able to pull it back on track.
- Reminding yourself of your goal is a hack that I often use. The goal is to train your mind and keep it within your control. Cogitating that from a higher perspective will allow your mind to focus on staying disciplined.

I'll end with a simple statistic and my perspective on it.

Roughly 70,000 thoughts run through our minds every day. Having a fully trained mind is essentially the ability to turn the maximum of those thoughts to our true and long-term advantage. If you can train your mind to do your bidding, you can make worlds collide. Ultimately, we know it is possible. After all, the world has witnessed great personalities such as Swami Vivekananda, who showed the world the power of training one's mind.

Before you go to the next chapter, here is a small exercise for you. Make a list of your goals. Once you do that, analyze and plan on how you are going to achieve them.

STEP -7

How to handle pressure in life?

> *"Stress acts as an accelerator: it will push you either forward or backward, but you choose which direction."*
>
> **- Chelsea Erieau**

Pressure and stress are inevitable, no matter how well-balanced your life is. While it is mostly perceived as a negative thing, if you know how to handle them properly, it can be a great force for you to push yourself. Yes, it is tricky, but it is important to achieve a balance and maintain a healthy relationship with the stress we will ultimately have to deal with in life. ***After all, coal turns into diamonds under pressure.***

Let's find out more about pressure, stress, and the different ways to deal with it.

Collapsing on her bed, Kala stared at the ceiling, utterly exhausted. The long day combined with the usual Monday stress had her feeling utterly drained. As she started to doze off, her email notification echoed through the room. Groaning, she reached for her phone and scrolled through the email, feeling her blood pressure spike with each word.

At the end of the week, however, when she finally completed all her work and stepped out of the office to enjoy her Friday night, she knew that without dealing with the pressure that came with life, she would have never gotten this far.

Our body is our home, the abode for all our diverse emotions, and putting it out there, working avidly to reach the apex of our potential can be stressful. And to top it all off are everyday triumphs and tribulations of life. But as Rudyard Kipling said,

"If we learn to keep our head when all around feels like losing ends, we can attain control of our perception and train ourselves in the right direction."

What is stress?

'I am so stressed, man.'

'Don't say that, I'll be stressed.'

'I didn't work today. This makes me stressed.'

'There is so much stress at home.'

I am sure we have all heard such sentences from people we know. But, what does stress actually mean? Does anyone have a clear definition of stress? Or do we just use the word as a synonym to being tense or having a bad day?

Stress has no well-defined notion attached to it.

Generally, it is our mental and physical reactions to adverse situations in life, and it differs from person to person. The cause of stress is a broad category and can be summarized under external and internal causes.

But is pressure always a bad thing?

Take a pressure cooker, for instance. When we cook rice, we wait for the whistle to blow, and the rice is cooked perfectly. Similarly, if we know how to handle stress and pressure, we can use it as a positive drive to achieve great things. Simply put, pressure is not the ordeal of life; it can be the driving force to bring out our potential, depending on how we see and take it. As Peter Marshall suggested,

"When we long for life without difficulties, remind us that oaks grow strong in contrary winds and diamonds are made under pressure."

So is stress necessary to be successful?

Just as a steady life is a secret to ultimate bliss, the success we strive to achieve is balanced in various aspects, and pressure is amongst its prominent retainers. **According to prominent psychologists, we are designed to stress when something we really care about is at stake, and it is the care that brings out our worthiness.**

Though stress and pressure can be beneficial, making the right balance is the key to achieving total potential and peace. It's okay to give your stress and pressure a home but never let this guest linger. But then, what happens if the guest lingers and takes over your home? How does stress impact your daily life?

If not balanced properly, the mere mention of stress can cause anyone to feel skittish and ill at once. In fact, stress and pressure in the wrong amounts can adversely impact our health mentally, physically, and emotionally, which in turn reduces our performance efficiency.

Coming from a working background and grinding my way to keep pace with the ambitious, high-achieving society, I can infer from my personal experience that pressure is inevitable. However, if we lose the rein and let it take the upper hand, it can hover and reduce us to just dragging our way everyday, with intense heaviness.

So how do we manage the right balance?

Well, this is where stress management steps in. To put it simply, I will make it simpler for you.

Why is it important to manage stress?

The straightforward answer is to secure and maintain a mental balance. Stress management is vital to ensure the limit of stress we are ready to endure in our life. Stress management aids in putting on a tight rein on the pressure in such a way that stress works only in the direction of driving you to perform with your full potential without taking a toll on your health and performance.

Therefore, with the options available, it is clear that the need of the hour is to deduce an action plan to handle pressure in life because the other pathway leads to devastation. In fact, why go for thorny bushes when you can settle for the charming fragrance of the situation? Here, I have enlisted some techniques that worked as guiding flames for me. Hopefully, they will enlighten your experience as well.

1. Master your thoughts

As we discussed before, when stress is managed in a balanced way, it can work wonders for you. According to many studies and research, balanced stress activates your cellular metabolism to active functioning.

- Channelize your thoughts in a positive direction.
- Find solutions rather than thinking about the problem.
- Take one step at a time

2. Understand your limitations

It is necessary to realize your limitations. In the fast-paced world, achieving the best in the shortest time is a constant pressure.

- However, you need to realize that too much strain breaks the steam; go at your pace, for it is better to bend than break.
- Be realistic, recognize your potential and align.

Because it doesn't matter if you go slow as long as you keep going.

- Sit back, reflect and go at your own pace.

3. Be optimistic

Positive thinking and attitude are fuel for our soul. However, by positive approach, I do not mean overlooking the problem.

- Problems and pressures are inevitable. However, it is seeking the solution that instills optimism.
- Try to collect yourself and then approach the situation with all possible outlooks, and you will get a solution to your problem.

4. Meditate

The mind is the master of the body. It can be your ally or nemesis, depending on how we train it.

- It is of utmost importance to calm your mind to gain an insightful understanding of your situation. And when it comes to achieving mental peace, meditation is the best arsenal.
- Make time for yourself, meditate and feed positive thoughts to your mind.

5. Organize and plan ahead

Approaching the challenges of life in an organized manner with a pre-planned action plan proves highly beneficial in managing pressure in life.

- Make a to-do list, prioritize your work and move ahead in a planned manner. Doing so will enhance your focus and cut out the extra noise.
- Have a do-it-now attitude, and do your work with zeal and enthusiasm.

6. Ask for help

There is no courage in taking all the burden, and there is no shame in asking for help. Neither of the two makes you more or less of a person.

- Asking for help when you are under too much pressure does not question or reduce your efficiency and abilities.
- Don't be afraid to reach out and ask for help.

7. Breathe, let go of negative thoughts.

Negative thoughts are often inescapable during adverse situations, particularly when you feel like the walls are closing on you.

- Stop, breathe and block out negative thoughts. In fact, sit back and take a break from thinking at all.
- Distract and calm yourself, and then dust yourself off to return to the mainstream.

Assemble your dreams, reflect on why you need to keep going despite the stumble, and move ahead. It is important to reach out for positivity. However, moving towards positivity should not be rushed; just keep your optimism all the time.

To sum it up, I'll end my perspective of pressure in a nutshell:

While striving to achieve and move ahead in life, stress and pressure will pose inevitable circumstances. However, only our attitude towards the same will decide whether it be a curse or a boon. So, no matter what, never give in to the situation and keep following your dreams

Before you go to the next chapter, here is a small exercise for you. Identify what stresses you out on a daily basis. Once you do that, try cutting out the negative pressure and take advantage of the positive pressure to achieve your goals.

STEP -8

How to handle personal disadvantages?

To every disadvantage, there is a corresponding advantage.

- W. Clement Stone

The saying is a cliché, but it's also true. Not everyone is born with a golden spoon, and sometimes, it becomes difficult to achieve your goals. But, if you look harder, you will realize that almost all successful people come from disadvantaged backgrounds. And how did they do this? They didn't let their disadvantages get the better of them. So the next time you struggle to overcome a disadvantage, remember that ***every obstacle you cross brings you closer to success.***

Let's find out more about how to overcome personal disadvantages and rise up successfully.

Kali felt a pang of envy as he watched his classmates getting dropped off by their parents or drivers. Born to poor parents, he could only dream of such a luxury. Though he was brilliant at his studies, he wasn't confident about getting anywhere in life and was resigned to remain as poor as his parents.

But that day, one of his teachers spoke about Sundar Pichai. Astonished that someone so famous and successful wasn't born rich changed something in him, and that day, he resolved to be as successful as he could become, come what may. And 15 years later, when he received the keys to his MERCEDES, he could imagine the little boy smiling in triumph.

It was Newton who gave the universal principle that every action has an equal and opposite reaction. It applies to this topic of discussion as well; let me explain how.

However, before anything else, maybe it would make sense to look at some of the finest examples of people who turned their personal disadvantages into advantages and, ultimately, conquered their fields.

Turning your weakness into strength

The first name that comes to mind is that of **Steve Jobs**. Dyslexic, he started a computer company out of his parent's garage and went on to create one of the greatest electronics brands in the history of the world.

The second name is ironic, the one who gave the world probably the greatest contribution to science – **Albert Einstein** was a scholar with a learning disability.

Fascinating, I know. But what allowed these people to move past their disadvantages or adversities and achieve a mantle that most of us only fantasize about achieving? While that may be a part of the answer, it is simply not the whole reality.

A common trait you'll find in nearly every successful person in the world is their ability to push through their disadvantages and adversities. No matter the situation, the adversity of the scenario, or the unpredictability of it, these great minds have always found a way to turn it, even if just by a little, to their advantage.

Is it difficult to learn this mentality? Absolutely.

Is it difficult in practice? Even more so than it is to learn.

Is it going to help me? Let's say that if it doesn't, you didn't do it right.

Before I tell you how you can overcome your personal disadvantages, I should probably explain what I mean when I say personal disadvantages. Now, a personal disadvantage generally refers to a personal loss or failure. For example, when I was younger, we didn't have much money. Therefore, pursuing the quality of education my peers (at present) got was not an option.

A personal disadvantage could be a disability of some sort added with an unpredictable circumstance at home, like the death of a loved one or a divorce. The point to remember about personal disadvantages is that it essentially varies from person to person. Something like being locked in a room may be an advantage to one, whereas to a claustrophobic, it would present itself as a terrifying disadvantage.

My point is that a personal disadvantage can be anything that sets a person back or at large, throws them off track. It can be trivial or simple, small or can be massive ; it doesn't matter. It's a disadvantage to be overcome, and the basic principles to do that remain the same.

So, what are these principles that I keep talking about?

1. Own it

I'll explain with an example from my personal experience. Coming from a middle-class family, I lacked the opportunity for fantastic education for my graduate studies and to grow my career. Rather than getting bogged down by my financial situation and continuing browsing options that were not feasible for me, I chose to face reality. I focused on improving everything that was within my control and would help me in my ultimate goal of being a successful individual.

- The first thing to do in a situation of personal disadvantage is to own the disadvantage.
- Do not dwell in denial. Denying it only makes the situation harder to overcome and , moreover it prevents you from doing anything productive about the situation.

The COVID 19 pandemic and lockdown posed personal disadvantages for almost everyone. However, was there anything that you could do to control this situation? No. So why wallow in the misery of it? Yes, you couldn't go to your place of work. But there's so much else that you could have done. You could have invested in upskilling courses, improved work efficiency, and worked from the comfort of your home!

2. Push through your situation

No matter what your situation is, it will pass. The grief after losing a close person can be debilitating but someday it too shall pass. The uncertainty about our future amidst this pandemic can be a jarring thought to deal with daily.

- Find a way, and push through your situation with your ultimate goal in your mind.
- If you don't have a specific goal in your mind, your ideal first step would be to decide upon a goal.
- Having done that, work towards it.

However, situations like these don't pass without you taking active action to correct or remedy them. Newton's First Law of Motion is that an object will remain at rest unless countered with an acting force.

So, if you're out of a job, you'll be out of a job unless you actively start looking for one. If you're stressed about completing a college submission, you'll continue to be stressed until you either start working on the application or till you finish it. No matter your situation, it will persist until you gather the courage or will to take action against it and push through the circumstance.

I have seen people fall out of jobs throughout this pandemic. I have seen people getting promoted. I have seen people fall out of a job, be in an undesirable financial and mental situation, and yet continue to grind until they have secured a new job.

Push. And keep pushing through your situation until you come out of the tunnel towards the light. Push until your disadvantage seems like a blip on your life's timeline.

3. Failure is your greatest teacher -

Thomas Alva Edison took his shot at creating a light bulb and became successful after multiple attempts. Keep in mind my use of the word 'attempt' and not failure. However, nobody cares about those thousand attempts. The world remembers him today for his invention of the electric bulb.

- Failure can be your greatest boon or your ultimate doom. For those people to whom failure seems like the end of the world, success will remain a fantasy because they have surrendered to failure.
- However, if you can harness the teachings from your failure, your next attempt might be more fruitful.

To put it into context, let's talk about examinations. Let's assume you want to become a CA. It is rare to find people in the profession that get certified in one attempt of the exam. But most successful CAs will tell you that it took them at least two tries to clear that examination.

Most successful CAs will also tell you that the teachings from the first attempt are what ultimately pushed them to improve in the second attempt.

My point is that being born with personal disadvantages was not in our hands. But staying in the situation created by those personal disadvantages is definitely a choice. These three principles that I have talked about have gotten not just me but countless people to the stature they occupy today. I would like to leave you with just this statement – it takes only one successful attempt to create history. So, no matter the adversity, keep trying with your ultimate goal in mind.

Before you go to the next chapter, here is a small exercise for you. Go back to a goal you gave up on because you kept failing. Figure out what went wrong, and get back to it to achieve success!

STEP -9

How to manage family expectations and personal ambitions?

> *There is no joy involved in following others' expectations of yourself*
>
> **- Miriam Toews**

On your path towards success, expectations and ambitions can make or break your game.Expectations from family, friends, and society are inevitable, it becomes hard to balance them with what we expect from ourselves. Our ambitions and desires are not always aligned with what is expected from us, and ***it takes great strength to break away and be true to your dreams and goals.***

A couple of weeks back, I met an old student of mine. I remember, when he started coaching with us, all he focussed on was 'who expected what from him'. He never worked or studied for himself but for the expectations of the world. Result of this was that he always felt burdened. I remember that I advised him to break free from external expectations and instead set goals that aligned with his true self. When I met him recently, it seemed the suggestion worked. He was doing very well in his career and was happy, without holding any burdens of expectations from others. That's the power of replacing expectations with tangible goals. Expectations are non-tangible, which means you can't measure them, while goals can be measured over a period of time.

Expectations are an essential and inescapable element of human existence. This guest needs no invitation to make themselves at home in your mind. Relationships, society, and our actuality survive on hope which in turn becomes expectations.

It is also necessary to understand that expectations are inevitable. It is completely up to you to let it make you or break you. Remember, expectations are like spices in food: the right amount promises wonders, whereas too much can lead to dysfunction in your system.

As Marilu Henner quoted,

"Being in control of your life and having realistic expectations about your day-to-day challenges are the keys to stress management, which is perhaps the most important ingredient to live a happy, healthy and rewarding life."

With the right balance, expectations can prove to be a blessing. So let us understand more about expectations and how to manage them with our ambitions.

Where do expectations come from?

Expectation arises from experience, communication, and emotions contributed by the surviving existence around us and ourselves. With the progression of life, we come across experiences at all turns, dressed as positive or negative impacts.

The word expectation comes from Latin vocable expectation, meaning "an awaiting." As humans, we possess a dire affinity for positivity. Adorned with hope, it becomes the foundation of expectations.

Hence, with unintentional influences or even explained beliefs regulating our life, expectations are inevitable. However, finding the right balance is essential to prevent unrealistic expectations ruining a peaceful life.

Difference between Healthy Expectations vs Unrealistic Expectations

Healthy expectations are the ideology and understanding to wish the best for someone but with equal respect to the individuality of others. Unrealistic expectations, however, basically work on the theory that people are obligated to anyone's ideas, with zero respect for individuality.

Healthy expectations allow you to not give in to the inevitable disappointment when expectation may lose its mark. For instance, consider the assumption and expectations we often set,to get back as much as we give in. Be it our parents, children, spouses, or any other relationships in our life: we often expect people to work along the line of action that resembles our input or thought process.

However, while it is perfectly okay to expect the bare minimum, it is equally important to understand and accept the concept of individuality. It is never worth your mental health to suffocate bonds with expectations.

Expand your horizon, and move ahead with the understanding that no one is obligated to fulfil your expectation. At the same time, prepare yourself to fall gracefully and learn with a strong will to keep going.

How do you manage personal expectations?

The journey to any bigger picture begins from within. So start by building an attitude that provides the best experience with personalised and disciplined service.

1. Value yourself

Skimming through the everyday struggles of life can be exhausting, especially if you are ruled by personal expectations.

- We are usually our biggest critics and tend to go harsh on ourselves, which isn't healthy. Personal expectations should be used as guiding allies to better ourselves.

- You may fall short at times, maybe more often than expected, but it's okay to stumble on your expectations as long as you possess the will to bounce back.
- Setbacks are lessons, not obstructions. Learn and move on.

2. Adaptation, the key to survival

Other than change, personal expectations are constant in our lives as well.

- With ever-changing times, ideologies and prospects, it is important to adjust your expectations.
- Sit back and reflect. Instead of carrying on with unrelenting expectations, adapt to the situation.
- Take a break, consider and anticipate according to the scenario.

3. Give time to understand healthy expectations and remove unrealistic assumptions

Holding an open-minded understanding of oneself is an absolute necessity.

- In order to keep pace or reach ambitious heights, we often project unrealistic expectations on ourselves. Moving ahead in healthy doses is the right way to proceed.
- Understand your timeline, live for the present, and most importantly, respect your personality.

- Coach your expectations to match with who you really are and not what you assume you are to fit in.

How do you manage outside expectations?

Nurturing personal presumptions is easier than handling expectations pitched our way from the outside. Though the right amount of expectation from family or friends can make us stronger, the wrong amounts impact us negatively as we allow them to impact our thoughts. This needs to stop by enforcing boundaries when necessary. Read on to enlighten yourself on how to manage other's expectations:

1. Communicate and make yourself heard

Growing up in a highly ambitious and achieving society, we are stumped with expectations from an early age.

- Don't give in to outside expectations. By accepting hardships today, we only sow difficulties for later.
- When even slightly doubtful, instead of giving in to unrealistic expectations to regret and suffer later, communicate and give voice to your thoughts.
- Muster the courage today to channel your best towards your actual potential tomorrow.

2. Set boundaries- It's okay to say no

No matter our expectations and opinions, we are often expected to align with the perspectives and ways of others.

- Do not give in; people will start taking advantage of

that. It is important to set boundaries and decline the prospects of others and choose yourself.

- Don't do anything because it's expected of you; do it only if you are prepared to do it.
- Prioritise yourself. Know your priorities and goals and move according to your outline for your growth, not how others want it for you.

3. Accept differences and let the burden lose

Despite clear communication from your side, sometimes people may not stop asserting their unrealistic expectations or reduce the burden of their expectations.

- Take a deep breath and let go. Remember, you can't influence others' negative thoughts and make them see the brighter side.
- Understand that most of the time, people are not open to a broader horizon, empathy, flexible thinking, or individuality.
- Consider and change your interactions with them, thereby cutting the binds of their expectations.

In the end, I would like to close on the note that excess of anything is bad. Without any doubt, expectation comes on top of the list. Find the right balance, and move ahead with your goals and ambitions with just-right amounts of expectation, both internal and external, for peaceful mental growth and health.

As a small exercise, create a list of expectations that you feel are pulling you back. In the other column, mention the tangible goals for them and replace the expectations with the goals.

STEP -10

Importance of Internships and Training

> *"Success isn't overnight. It's when everyday you get a little better than the day before. It all adds up."*
>
> **– Dwayne Johnson**

Experience is an important part of success. Whether good or bad, they help build our knowledge and repertoire to meander our way through life. In terms of career, internships fill that role, especially if you are a student. While many do it for marks or their resume, with the right internship, you can easily gain the upper hand in the industry that you want to make a mark in.

Let's learn about internships and their importance in building a successful career.

One of my mentees once asked me, 'Why should I take an internship?'

That's a million-dollar question.

Internships definitely look great on a resume. But is that the only purpose of taking up an internship? Is there no real-world benefit to those countless hours slogging under your seniors and other professionals? This chapter will help you uncover the answers to these questions.

What is an internship?

This is the first question that comes to mind when the topic of internships strikes in.

Simply put, an internship refers to temporary employment offered to students or professionals to boost their competence and understanding of their respective fields.

Temporary Employment for Experience: Internships are typically short in tenure, where the interns can absorb as much knowledge about their field as possible while incorporating experiential and hands-on learning techniques.

Gaining Practical Knowledge: For example, an interning doctor is expected to accompany a surgeon into the Operation Theater. Even though they may not actually work on the operation, it is their job to gain as much knowledge about the procedure, complications and the know-how of an operation and the tools used in the procedure.

Similarly, a legal intern is expected to learn and understand the culture within a law firm and learn how their employer or senior works on their cases. They are expected to learn by carrying out experiential work such as the drafting of various documents or preparing briefs, or simply offering their arguments and observations regarding an active case.

Types of Internships:

The purpose, across all fields, is primarily to learn about a person's respective field. Now, there are essentially two types of internships – paid and unpaid.

Paid Internships: As the name suggests, paid internships are internship opportunities that pay their interns for the work they handle, not in the form of a salary, but rather as a stipend or something that offers an incentive to the intern to deliver quality work.

The vast majority of times, a stipend is very less compared to the average salaries of a full-time employee in that field. However, since an intern's purpose is to learn, this is deemed acceptable.

Unpaid Internships: On the other hand, an unpaid internship is one where there is no form of monetary remuneration for the intern. Rather, the complete focus is on offering quality exposure and imparting knowledge to the intern.

Typically, students take unpaid internships in their respective fields to improve their professional worth or finish a degree rather than as a means to earn money. In general, most internships have tenures of 1 month that can extend up to 1 year.

How does experiential learning help?

Internships prepare a candidate for better placements

in terms of employability. It helps the interns to prepare for the real-world scenarios and teaches them the best way to tackle those scenarios as well. This is essentially what experiential learning refers to. When anybody learns with experience, they would more likely be able to hold on to that learning as compared to picking it up from a book.

The concept of experiential learning

The concept of experiential learning has been around for a long time. First proposed by David Kolb, a psychologist, it was said that experiential learning was the process where knowledge is created through the transformation of experience. That knowledge is a result of combinations of grasping and transforming that experience.

With the industry becoming increasingly skill-oriented, experiential learning plays a role of utmost importance in imbibing these skills into prospective industry members by allowing them to gain experience in the nitty-gritty of their respective fields. The basic advantages offered by experiential learning are –

1. Better grasp on concepts -

Rather than reading texts about a concept, when interns are allowed to witness a particular scenario or object of study in the real world, it is easier for the intern to understand the processes and various aspects of the concept.

2. Creativity is encouraged -

Instead of sticking to a prescribed procedure for solving a problem, real-world experiential learning allows students to use their skills to figure out the best way to solve the problem.

3. Retrospection and introspection lead to increase in learning value -

When students make mistakes, they not only reflect upon the reasons, but they also think about the various other ways of handling the situation. This allows a fostering of quality learning that they can continue to carry forward into their professional lives.

Why should you intern?

Now that we know,internships offer crucial real-world experience in your respective professional field, let us understand what other reasons there are for you to look for internship opportunities.

1. Opens up a plethora of opportunities -

The fact is that once you've gained some internship experience anywhere, you are closer to being the ideal candidate for an internship elsewhere.

- When you've sought multiple experiences from several internships, you are essentially prepared for most of the things that the professional world will throw at you.

- Having multiple internships in your resume plays an important role in making your resume as one that stands out amongst the average fresher.

2. Professional as well as personal development -

As an intern, you will be made to step out of your comfort zone and work in real-time situations.

- As a result, they gain crucial work ethics and a hard-working mentality that is bound to help them in the long run, regardless of whether it is in the professional aspects of their life or personal.
- The character growth they gain will influence the way they will live all through their life.

3. Networking -

In today's professional spheres, networking plays a role of unparalleled importance due to the kind of exposure it helps you to secure.

- The first step to networking, for most people, is through internships. For example, a law student performs well at an internship with an advocate who deals with civil matters and gradually they develop a professional trust upon one another.. Five years later, if the student becomes a criminal advocate, owing to their professional proximity, a lot of work can be referred to by their senior.
- Similarly, if an engineering student interns at a big

company and builds a healthy professional relationship with the team there, then after graduating, they can get opportunities through the company.The chances of securing a contract or opportunity with the company you interned with are substantially higher since you have an existing and mutually beneficial relationship with them.

4. Learn more than the bare minimum required for your profession -

Most courses teach us only the core subject matter of any field. However, there are countless corollaries that most of us remain unaware of until we start working.

- For an engineer, dealing with software, it is equally crucial for them to understand how an engine works.
- Similarly, an architect should be able to understand how to secure a contract as well as know how to sketch the design plan.
- These industry lessons can only be learned with experience, and internships seek to offer this experience.

An internship training experience allows you to become a well-rounded professional equipped with the technical knowledge along with the soft skills and knowledge of corollary processes that allow any project to come to life.

The fact that internships look good on a resume

is simply a benefit for students learning in real-time situations. Whenever an intern selects or scouts for internships, it must be to boost knowledge and skill rather than chasing a certificate that holds no real value.

Before you go to the next chapter, here is a small exercise for you. Make a profile on LinkedIn, and start applying for internships relevant to your field.

STEP -11

How do you score marks in the examination of your choice?

> *"Success is the sum of small efforts, repeated day in and day out."*
>
> **-Robert Collier**

Exams are tough, but anticipating your marks after is almost torture. Did I do well? Are my marks enough to qualify for the entrance? While marks are important, it is equally necessary to be consistent to score well without succumbing to pressure. Scoring marks may be important for your future, but learning along the way is essential for your success.

Let's find out more about how to score well, and the habits that will help you do so with minimal stress.

Raunak sat in his seat, terrified. As Manish sir slammed his physics paper on his desk and walked away, he closed his eyes and took a deep breath. Tentatively, he opened his eyes and looked at his score. He had failed. As his brain tried to process the information, his vision started going black at the edges. As the darkness crept in, a ringing sound penetrated his consciousness…

Raunak sat up in his bed , eyes wide open and heart racing wildly with fear. Realizing it was only a dream, he sighed and flopped back on his bed, exhausted. Though he was a topper, the necessity of scoring well in every exam caused a lot of pressure and anxiety. He wished he could take it easy, but it was impossible.

Five minutes later, his alarm blared again, and he groaned. Reaching over and shutting it off, he trudged over to his desk and opened his Physics book, determined not to let his horrifying dream become a reality.

The harsh truth is that every student is confronted with the necessity of scoring good marks in their educational journey . Marks play an integral role in deciding your future, even if one ignores their importance, marks still hold the basis that defines how much hard work you will need to put in the future to make your career. Not only do marks pave the way for colleges and courses of your choice, but they also show your future employers certain qualities expected of an employee, such as the will to work hard.

Having said that, most students either face this harsh reality by themselves or learn because of external factors such as one's parents and teachers reinforcing the same onto them. If you are reading this right now, you are probably hoping to find a solution to improve your marks, which means that you have already accepted that marks are important for the future. This has been written to help students further their intention of scoring well in any examination of their choosing.

What are the best techniques you can use to score above 90% marks in your examination?

The first thing students must remember is that most of the time, scoring above 90% in an examination is not solely about working hard. Working smart not only reduces the amount of labor a student needs to do but also substantially boosts his chances of scoring well in the exam. Now, smart work is a habit or discipline that students must incorporate into their schedules to be able to score as much as they want. Keep reading to find out more about these strategies by which students can work smartly and achieve their goal of scoring above 90% in their examination.

1. Proper time management techniques

The most successful people in the world consider efficient time management as one of the prime methods to achieve success.

- A student's daily schedule should consist of what to study and the specifics of what they wish or require to learn.
- Modulate the study durations according to subject difficulty and prioritize according to their importance

in the examination.

- The easiest way for time management is to create a timetable or a routine chart that includes proper breaks between studying.

2. A long-term study schedule

It is neither easy nor advisable for a student to start studying at the last minute in an unplanned, haphazard manner if they wish to score above 90% in an examination.

- Create a study plan that outlines the topics that need to be covered with ample time for revisiting or revising important topics for an examination.
- Ideally, allocate about one day for one topic and leave ample time for solving sample and previous years' question papers before the actual examination.

3. Competing with ones' self

In preparing for an examination, students must strive to compete with themselves daily while aiming to achieve more than what they could do previously.

- While preparing for exams, try to decrease the time it takes to solve problems without compromising accuracy.
- This boosts overall productivity so that students can improve their work quality.
- Students should set small and achievable targets to avoid getting demotivated in the long run.

4. Addressing topics that a student struggles with

Provided the student has started preparing well in advance, students must first try and grasp the topics that they find difficult.

- For example, if organic chemistry is a difficult subject for a student, they should devote more time and effort to understanding that subject.
- However, students should start preparing with plenty of time left to complete the syllabus before the examination date for effective results.

5. Learn rather than rote-learning

Many students resort to rote learning their study material to attempt and score good marks.

- However, with rote learning, concept-based subjects like physics or math will be difficult to answer and solve.
- Rote learning prevents the students from applying their knowledge of the subject in answering it.
- Moreover, understanding the core concepts and fundamentals of a subject of study will enable students to remember the concepts better.

6. Study smart

There is no point in devoting an equal amount of time to two topics when they are not equally important for the examination.

- Students must focus on improving their understanding of topics that are bound to be asked in an exam rather than topics only worth a few marks.
- Give weightage to the topics that have more chance of appearing in your exams.
- However, the ideal scenario is that students try to complete the whole syllabus well in advance so that the need for selective study does not arise in the first place.

7. Don't shy away from helping peers -

Some students believe that explaining topics and difficulties to their peers is a waste of time.

- However, research has proven that explaining a concept allows the person teaching to secure a firmer grasp of that concept.
- Helping someone learn offers a chance to introspect and analyze that topic in-depth while explaining it to a second or third person.
- However, students must strike a balance between studying for themselves and helping their peers.

8. Revise sample and previous years' question papers

Revising and solving previous years' question papers is important and cannot be stressed enough for a student aiming to score above 90%.

- Revision allows students to thoroughly analyze their learnings in a subject and cover any topics they might have missed the first time they covered the topic.
- After revising, students should solve the previous year's question papers to allow students to apply their learnings in an examination..
- Students can start solving question papers after the first round of revision.
- As they get more confident, they can even time themselves according to the timing of the actual examination.
- Revising helps students to improve their performance under pressure similar to one of an actual examination.

Following these tips and tricks will help students to score marks above 90% in any given examination of their choosing if followed properly. Devote ample amounts of time for physical exercise and rest. Students often neglect other aspects of their lifestyle when preparing for an examination, considering it a waste of time.

However, there is a plethora of research that has proved that if the body is healthy, then the mind will function better. The last thing any student would want is to burn out and lose confidence and motivation to score the required marks for one's career. Having said that, we wish students all the very best and hope that this brings them at least a step closer to scoring well and achieving their dreams.

STEP -12

How to build your personality and a mindset for life?

> *"Once your mindset changes, everything on the outside will change along with it."*
>
> **-Steve Maraboli**

While appearances are important, it is important to have an attractive personality and mindset to build a successful life for yourself. While our looks contribute to our first impression, it will not last without an equally good personality. So, keep working on yourself and grow into becoming someone who inspires others with their being.

Let's find out more about how to build a good mindset and personality.

There are countless ways to improve the standard of your life, mentally, spiritually, and physically without compromising on the quantitative metrics of success.. One such way is to build an attractive personality. At the outset, it is crucial to remember that nobody is immune to change. All you need to effectuate is that change in a positive direction is good and that to work towards your goal, it is extremely important.

The American Psychology Association defines a personality as the individual differences in characteristic patterns of thinking, feeling, and behaving. In simple words, one's personality is the core of his psychology or his idiosyncratic characteristics. Your personality is built on different components of your behavior, such as your instincts, the way you think, feel, and behave in different situations.

While physical appearance is often mistaken to be a person's personality, it is merely a part of it. Appearance can be an important aspect of your personality, but your personality trumps your physical appearance.

Thus, while building an attractive or desirable personality is a long-term pursuit, here are some of the basic practices you can begin to incorporate into your daily life that will help you to inculcate these changes easily.

1. Listen before you speak

To listen is one of the first things we are taught as kids, and for a good reason.

- Without listening to your surroundings and social circle, nothing you say or want to say will ever be relevant or appreciable. A human being is a social animal, and animals need to communicate.
- To communicate effectively, listen to the person speaking with you before you wish to add to something they say.

- Not only does this allow the person in front of you to speak comfortably, but also allows them to appreciate the fact that you are listening to what they have to say rather than adding irrelevant speech as a rebuttal to what they say.
- Being a good listener allows you to glean more information from the happenings around you and in turn, makes it easier for you to relate to your circumstances or surroundings.
- Practice targeted listening daily in every conversation you have, whether it's with your employer or your date.

2. Broaden your scope of knowledge

Frankly, to come across as a person of authority or a personality that compels attention (in the positive sense), they must invest in a constant pursuit to broaden their scope of knowledge.

- By itself, this is a practice that reserves multiple benefits, a few of which are that it allows a person to stay sharp, improve their analytical skills, and learn new things, which could lead to the development of related interests and boost their creativity.
- Once you broaden your scope of knowledge, you will find yourself speaking with more authority with people who have already established some level of dominance in those fields.

- If nothing else, this is a practice that will make you the smartest person in most rooms.

3. Conversation goes hand in hand with listening

Imagine a situation where you are speaking with a person, and they say nothing in response or merely utter a few unmeaningful words here and there. Would that be a conversation you'd want to invest your time in? No.

- Nobody wants to be speaking 'at' someone rather than 'with' someone. Now, imagine another situation where you are conversing with a person who listens to you and contributes meaningfully.
- Generally, this would be a conversation everybody would want to enjoy because it is constructive.
- Therefore, once you start listening effectively and have started making an effort to improve your scope of knowledge, you must put them to good use and build quality conversations, no matter who you're speaking with.

4. Improve your social circle

Improving not only the quality of one's social circle but also the quantity of that quality goes a long way in molding an attractive personality and mindset.

- Being around people that challenge you to improve yourself propel you towards growth.
- For some people, this improvement comes out of peer pressure, and for others, it comes out of a desire for

self-improvement.

- Regardless of how you meet that goal, the quality and quantity in your social circle push you toward it.
- Engaging with bright minds allows you to mold a mindset desirable for a compelling personality.

5. Be strong

A common quality in every desirable personality is the ability to hold your ground for things that matter to you.

- To inculcate this aspect of personality, your morality must be the right kind.
- However, holding off any undue pressure about things that are simply wrong plays a crucial role in establishing the fact that you have mental resilience.
- Practice being unwavering when the person in front of you is morally wrong. Over time, this will become a part of your regular personality.

6. Appreciate things that deserve appreciation

It is undesirable to be around a person who constantly complains about every other thing around them.

- A person needs to appreciate the things in life that deserve appreciation.
- Not only will this practice allow you to be happier, but more centered and confident about yourself.
- There is a positive to every negative in the world, so why only focus on the negatives?

7. Respect the people around you

What goes around comes around, and the same adage applies to respect.

- You will be respected by your peers and the people surrounding you if you treat them with the appropriate amount of respect in every situation.
- If you can respect the people around you, the people around you will be more inclined to respect you.
- Even though this seems trivial, respect is one aspect of a personality that is inherent in every great personality of the world.

8. Practice empathy

What makes every personality an approachable one is its ability to empathize with the emotions of its audience.

- No matter the situation, showing empathy to the person going through it could make their day. Remember that empathy is not the same as sympathy, and not many people appreciate sympathy.
- Practicing empathy regarding seemingly trivial situations goes a long way in allowing yourself to develop into a better human being and, consequently, a stellar personality.

9. Practice your soft skills

Soft skills go a long way in making a great impression on people.

- Little things like having a firm handshake, being well-spoken in whichever language of your choice, carrying yourself with a good posture, and paying attention to hygiene and appearance are important.
- Being appropriate and relevant in any given context all build up to form inalienable parts of one's personality.

10 Find comfort in yourself

None of these practices will be of any use in your pursuit of developing a good personality if you cannot be comfortable in your skin.

- Your mindset must be that of self-love, and while you must try to keep growing as a person, being overly critical of yourself is a confidence-depleting habit and must be avoided in excess.
- If you are comfortable with yourself, your personality will come across as one of self-assurance and confidence – great traits for a great personality!

Where there is a will, there is a way. Regardless of your starting point, there will always be scope for improvement. In order to achieve great heights of success, one must consistently work on improving his mindset and personality. Practicing the aforementioned points one at a time will gradually make it the person's nature and ultimately improve the person's personality.

STEP -13

Transitioning from Learner,s life to real-life

> *The best way to predict your future is to create it*
>
> **- Abraham Lincoln**

The beauty of life is how it always keeps changing. Childhood, student life, and finally, adulting; by the time you look back, your life's trajectory would resemble a thrilling roller coaster ride. And the most trying period would be the transition from student to adult life. Learning to function as a full-fledged adult can be terrifying, but with the right attitude and mindset, you can grow into a wiser and more mature person over the years.

Let's find out about transitioning from benches to office desks, and how to handle it.

Amit grinned as he tossed his graduation cap up in the air along with dozens of others. Laughing along with his friends, he looked around the campus. Memories of lectures, skipping classes for a samosa, hanging out with friends, cramming for semesters, and running behind professors to get their projects finished, all came rushing back, and for a moment, fear gripped his heart. He was no longer a carefree student; he had a job and bills to pay.

And then, he remembered what his favourite professor Dr. Manoj had told him on the last day of college: the worst thing that can happen to you is when you stop moving and become stagnant in life.

Life is a never-ending transition. Right from the beginning, our life progresses from chapter to chapter to finish our story. Though all stages are equally mysterious and compelling, the transition from student life to real-life beholds quite a significant part.

A Learner's Life

A Learner's Life involves lifelong friendships, rebellious independence, a carefree attitude, and many fun, lighthearted experiences. But one day, you wake up and realise you are now an adult, which means you try to get an insightful vision of what 'adulting' really is. And that entails a crucial change. Change, though constant, can be hard too; you can either drag it along or master it.

As a learner/student, your major worries are grades and maintaining your attendance. Towards the end, your priority changes to finding a job or pursuing higher education. And then, boom! You suddenly find yourself working, and the numbers are reflected on your bank account instead of your grade sheet.

The transition can be overwhelming, but in reality, your life as a student is an impromptu training session that helps you face real life.

However, to handle and master any situation, insightful knowledge always rewards you with an edge, so let us begin with the obvious question,

How is student life different from work-life?

To begin with, one of the biggest contrasts between work-life and student life is that you acquire a broader sense of freedom and independence. You are finally facing reality in a highly ambitious and fast-paced world. While you are rewarded for your efforts with grades as a student, you are paid for your efforts as a working adult.

However, with money and independence comes responsibilities. Though student life has its share of commitments, they increase several folds during work life. In fact, work-life disciplines your schedule, making you more focused and responsible.

What is a major change from student life to work life?

Another unmistakable distinction in work life is the individuals and the environment. Though competition is equally prevalent in student life, lifelong amigos are no foreign concepts in this phase of life. In fact, it is generally the final stage where genuine friendships are formed. In the case of work-life, the competition shadowed by clouds of professionalism is highly pervasive. Besides, associating outside work is quite tiring due to personal commitments.

However, both student life and work-life share a similarity; your efforts are always evaluated. You receive feedback both as a student and a professional, though the stakes and consequences are higher in the real world.

Are there any tricks to a successful student to work life transition?

Work and school life are diverse in numerous angles, embellished with their share of hardships and rewards. However, when you transition from student life to real life, the mental pressure is inescapable and real. Though there are no particular or explicit rules to guide your way through the transition nonetheless, knowing the basic groundwork always helps. Remember, planning is always the strategy to proceed. But planning comes with the idea of what lies ahead.

As Yvon Chouinard said,

"Fear of the unknown is the greatest fear of all."

And with that comes the next question,

"What are the challenges that one may face while moving from student life to work-life?"

Moving from student life and entering a fast-paced, high-achieving environment is undoubtedly a roller coaster ride. Nevertheless, a combination of flexibility, openness to change, and willingness to embrace and adapt to opportunities is the fuel to conquer the transitional ride. So, fasten your seatbelts and read on to identify the challenges that may obstruct the way of your navigation.

1. Money:

More often than not, we have heard that money can't buy happiness. Though it is true in a sense, money is a basic necessity needed to support your livelihood. And when you become responsible for your expenses, proceeding in the right way and budgeting can be quite taxing.

- Making money and paying for yourself can be overwhelming and terrifying at the same time. However, you would feel independent and grow as a person.
- Additionally, figuring out the right balance and discovering what you need and what you can manage is another piece of the post-school expectation you learn.

2. Broader and a new range of social exposure:

As students, we can be carefree and largely ruled by companionship. You come across groups sharing your ideologies or interests, making it easier to get along. However, in the real and ambitious world, everyone wants to be the best and achieve everything.

- The competition is way too high with literally no span to sit back and chill.
- Work-life calls for strict professionalism, particularly if you want to go far in the long race.

- However, it is also a great place for learning; with professionals from different backgrounds and varying experiences, the work-life opens a Pandora to great learning experiences.

3. Responsibility:

Transitioning from student life to real life brings forth a plethora of responsibilities. Gone are the days of procrastination, careless outlook, and undisciplined schedules. As you navigate the real world, you become answerable for your actions.

- You can no longer take days off just like that. As an adult, your leaves are supervised and limited.
- Work procedure, execution, and outlook are monitored and rewarded accordingly. With real-world adulting comes the responsibility of being answerable for your actions.

Nevertheless, sometimes even though you may wish to stamp out the welcome sign, the transitions are inevitable. Therefore, preparations are the best way to go along; a light push with proper guidance can always help to trace your tracks. Read on to discover some ways to make a smooth transition from student life to work life.

1. Accept the idea of change:

As we all know, change is the only constant-prepare yourself for the ideology of transition. Life is a series of transitions. We all know we have to grow up someday.

- Take responsibility and proceed ahead. No good comes out of procrastinating the inevitable.
- Face the change and adapt. Weekdays call for focused and disciplined executions.
- To achieve personal growth in a peaceful mental state, organisation, focus, and discipline are the mantras of your new transition stage.

2. Deduce a structure that compliments you:

As a student, your flow is directed and guided by the institution that builds your personal growth. Right from semesters, syllabus, assignments, and exams, you know the route to enhance your personal growth. However, this drastically changes in the real world.

- In the case of work-life, you get to carve your way. Your dream job, the way to secure it, and progress in the field while managing your personal life depends on you entirely.
- Thus, decide and settle on what's best for you, not where the herd is moving.

3. Move ahead with an open mind and patience:

As an outsider, you may hold a perspective of the working world you are about to enter, and that's okay as long as you are flexible. With so many factors such as teachers, seniors, parents, or social platforms, you are easily subject to influence.

- Knowledge is good; recognize what you are doing. However, instil flexibility. Move ahead with an open mindset as work-life exposes you to a world of varying experiences and people.
- Align to adding knowledge to your ideas with the acceptance of learning at all ends.
- Be patient; you will face diverse experiences, and some may leave you disappointed. Just learn from them and keep moving.
- At times, you may go unappreciated. However, remember it's not the end; as long as you keep going, you are still in the race.
- Reflect on the falls, sharpen your tools and move ahead with motivation and patience.

4. Start with low-key expectations:

Rome was not built in a day. The idea of adulting is often glamorised, but remember that's just the virtual world.

- In real life, when you transition into work-life, you enter as a novice. You won't run for president on day one. So, move ahead with readjusted expectations.
- Sharpen your edges with learning and take small baby steps to navigate from student life to work life.

5. Be your friend:

Taking the hard way is never the right way. Be your

own friend, and guide yourself to restrain from taking pressure and stress.

- When everything is going downhill with too much mental traffic, reach out for help. Communicate and talk to figure out if there is some way.
- Transitions can be hard, especially when you don't have the experience to face them. It's perfectly fine to stumble even right at the start.
- A peaceful and healthy mind yields higher efficiency, so be your friend and help yourself through the transition.

I would conclude on the note that with the right outlook, preparation and coordination, even the hardest transitions will be smooth. The prime objective is to deduce a balance between peaceful mental status and important activities to accomplish an efficient transition from student life to real life. In fact, you will eventually want to galvanise towards this new experience.

As a small exercise, write down what you feel work life would be like. Once done, talk to your parents or other working friends and bust the myths and wrong facts on your list.

STEP -14

Prepare yourself for a Successful Life

Success is not final; failure is not fatal: It is the courage to continue that counts

- Winston S. Churchill

No matter how big or small the task, we always do them with the intent of finishing them successfully. Success is achieved with hard work, determination, discipline, and persistence. Yes, it is easy to get discouraged, but you will face eternal disappointment if you give up easily. While you may fail at some point, as long as you keep pushing past those obstacles, nothing will stop you from ultimately reaching your destination.

Let's find out how to plan and prepare for success.

Success is the ultimate goal of even the most basic and modest implementations of life. Every action thrives towards the conclusive design of success. Be it your relationships, career, health, or happiness: you often proceed with the primary aim of achieving the best.

However, it is also important to remember that success is the trophy of a long-lasting marathon. Life is built on the tracks running through numerous twists and turns. To survive and reach our ultimate goals of successful existence, it is absolutely necessary to master the elemental constituents such as persistence, hard work, commitment, and discipline to win.

Success is the elemental practice of desire in combination with determination to succeed. Abilities and skills are pointless if they aren't exercised with planning and practice. Both these attributes go hand in hand to guide your way to success. One without the other is similar to food without water. To nurture success, both are equally important. In simple words, planning for success is nothing without preparing for success.

However, one might wonder what the difference is between the two.

How is 'planning for success' different from 'preparing for success'?

To answer this question, we reflect on the basic definition of the same; planning is the layout that you sketch, weighing your assets and falls to contrive the map to reach your goal. While preparation is getting ready with practice and exercising to execute your plan. One without the other is a total waste on the other hand disciplined planning with preparation works wonders.

In real life, we have little control over what falls our way. As such, planning sometimes may go off the hill, and in such scenarios, it is only preparation that saves the day. Planning gets you started, and preparation rewards you with the extra edge to succeed. Planning a delicious treat may get you off your couch. However, the right preparation brings forth the triumph of scrumptious food.

However, what needs to be considered here is that success is a broad-ranged concept. Desire, determination, hard work, planning, and execution are among the numerous milestones of this long voyage. Having said that, while conquering success is a long-term pursuit, here are some basic practices for you to incorporate and implement in your strategy while preparing yourself for a life of success:

1. Burning desire

Desire is the elemental attribute, to begin with. And when the stakes are as high as the aim and vision of achieving the best, frail inclinations are easily vanquished.

- A small flame may light a candle. However, it is not enough to illuminate a fire torch. Similarly, beginning with weak willingness extinguishes the journey long before its proper spread.
- However, when you are scintillating with a burning desire adorned with firm determination and discipline, the starting point pushes you to greater lengths and directions of accomplishing your action plans.

Change your focus

One of the profound obstructions in the path of

success is fear. The fear of failure or loss can be highly deteriorating; it eats away your potential to proceed.

- Change your focus; plan to win rather than not to lose. As the saying goes, "Shoot for the Moon. Even if you miss, you will land among the stars".
- Failure is never the enemy. It can be your ally, depending on your perspective. However, remember that the lack of effort is your real nemesis.
- When you proceed under the pressure of failure, you start from a position of weak grounds. Your efforts lack their full potential and can easily succumb to the piling pressure as you move ahead.
- Focus on proceeding with inspiration, not desperation.

Emphasis on Commitment

Motivation nudges you to set about. However, it is the commitment that keeps you going. As Jean-Paul Sartre rightly said,

"Commitment is an act, not a word."

- In simple words, commitment is the willingness and integrity combined with rock-solid intent and focus on carrying out a course of action plan or purpose throughout the hindering obstructions.
- With ardent commitment, you focus on playing to win not to avoid the fear of losing. And when you focus on winning, you prepare harder.

- Remember, no situation will be ideal, success will demand a high price, so whether you drift along or against the wind, the important part is determination and to keep going with commitment.

Enhance your knowledge as you proceed

Opening with the words of Arthur Ashe,

"Success is a journey, not a destination. The doing is often more important than the outcome".

The next crucial aspect of the action plan that equips you for the expedition of success is the journey itself.

- As you go forward on your path to achieve and conquer your dreams, life through diverse experiences comes your way. Whether these experiences are exhilarating or devastating, sometimes they find a middle ground.
- However, one common prospect each experience in life bestows is the lesson you learn. It is on you to recognize and understand the silver lining.
- Enhance your knowledge, focus on the journey, learn from your mistakes and get back in the game with greater potential.

Power of persistence

The voyage of success is never easy. Even the basic planning and preparation for a life of success is full of setbacks.

- When preparing for a life of success, persistence is an

important tool with the combination of various other attributes.

- Hurdles and falls are inevitable. However, the willingness to brush off and bounce back strengthens your action plan.
- When you miss the mark, quitting is the easy way out, but your endurance makes you a winner.
- Often, people lose because they choose the easy way and quit; however, pain and purpose fuel persistence, which ultimately drives you to success.

Avoid distractions

When you move ahead on your journey to achieve great results, distractions rush in to hinder your path.,

- Recognize and discard the meaningless aspects and shift your focus to challenges and learning.
- Enlist the things that waste your time and stand firm to avoid these distractions.

Build a positive attitude

Attitude plays an important role when you are preparing to attain success.

- A positive attitude is often confused with negligence of proper acknowledgment of the problem.
- Remember, a positive attitude is not about turning a blind eye to a problem. In fact, it is more about being solution-focused.

- A positive mindset is a supplement to your action plan, not a substitute.

Strategize

Remember, you are building an enthralling empire, and the layout is a basic necessity.

- Plan out and prepare your when, what, and how for at least four days ahead. You do not need to stress about the future.
- However, prepare for your immediate tomorrow. Strategizing provides an insight into the action plan and prepares you to face the future on strengthening grounds.

Be your greatest asset and ally

This is your journey, don't rely on others to figure out and achieve your goals for you.

- While it is perfectly fine to look up to others for emotional support, it's also beneficial to avoid the habit of dependency.
- When you go out in the real world, you will be facing the circumstances alone. Therefore, build a habit of independence.
- Strengthen your will and believe in yourself.

Avoid burnout

Planning and thriving to achieve your goal is crucial; however, securing a balance to avoid your vision turning into obsession is equally important and necessary.

- Zero in on your objective; however, don't fixate on it. Keep yourself productive and proactive with a balanced touch of fun and relaxation.
- Contrive ways to grow, however, not at the stake of your mental peace.
- A healthy mind is a key to a healthy existence, which is ultimately the highway to efficient working and great results.

In the end, I would conclude on the note that the strategies to prepare yourself for a life of success are not rocket science. With firm willingness, anyone can master them. We all have hidden treasures within us; all it needs is deep reflection and recognition. Start today, recognize your strengths, and learn what it takes to achieve a life of success. Remember, there is no substitute for planning, preparation, hard work, and persistence.

"As you reach the end of this book, remember that success is not just a destination; it is a journey of perseverance, resilience, and unwavering determination. Embrace every challenge as an opportunity to grow, and every setback as a lesson in disguise. Believe in the power of your dreams, for they have the potential to shape your reality. Let this book be the catalyst that ignites your drive to reach new heights and conquer the impossible. You have within you the strength and tenacity to create your own definition of success. Keep striving, keep believing, and keep pushing forward. Your story of success has only just begun."